CIVIC VIRTUE
LET'S WORK TOGETHER

HOW TO PROMOTE THE COMMON GOOD

JOSHUA TURNER

PowerKiDS press™

New York

Published in 2019 by The Rosen Publishing Group, Inc.
29 East 21st Street, New York, NY 10010

First Edition

Editor: Melissa Raé Shofner
Book Design: Tanya Dellaccio

Photo Credits: Cover JGI/Tom Grill/Blend Images/Getty Images; p. 4 Dimitrios/Shutterstock.com; p. 5 Paul Bradbury/OJO Images/Getty Images; p. 7 wavebreakmedia/Shutterstock.com; p. 8 (George Washington) https://commons.wikimedia.org/wiki/File:Gilbert_Stuart_Williamstown_Portrait_of_George_Washington.jpg; p. 9 (U.S. Constitution) https://commons.wikimedia.org/wiki/File:Constitution_of_the_United_States,_page_1.jpg; p. 9 (classroom) Monkey Business Images/Shutterstock.com; p. 11 littlenySTOCK/Shutterstock.com; p. 13 (Obama signs) Bloomberg/Getty Images; pp. 13 (people in meeting), 22 Rawpixel.com/Shutterstock.com; p. 15 Victorian Traditions/Shutterstock.com; p. 17 (top) Simon Ritzmann/Photodisc/Getty Images; p. 17 (bottom) Cory Seamer/Shutterstock.com; p. 19 Cincinnati Museum Center/Archive Photos/Getty Images; p. 20 VGstockstudio/Shutterstock.com; p. 21 Drew Angerer/Getty Images News/Getty Images.

Cataloging-in-Publication Data

Names: Turner, Joshua.
Title: How to promote the common good / Joshua Turner.
Description: New York : PowerKids Press, 2019. | Series: Civic virtue: let's work together | Includes glossary and index.
Identifiers: LCCN ISBN 9781508166887 (pbk.) | ISBN 9781508166863 (library bound) | ISBN 9781508166894 (6 pack)
Subjects: LCSH: Ethics–Juvenile literature. | Social ethics–Juvenile literature. | Social advocacy–Juvenile literature.
Classification: LCC BJ1012.T87 2019 | DDC 170–dc23

Manufactured in the United States of America

CPSIA Compliance Information: Batch #CS18PK: For Further Information contact Rosen Publishing, New York, New York at 1-800-237-9932

CONTENTS

THE COMMON GOOD

When you think about what's good for you, you might think of getting a new toy, eating your favorite food, or playing a game with your friends. When you think about something that's good for your class, you might think of going on a field trip or watching a movie.

But what about something that's good for everyone? When something is good for everyone—no matter where they come from, who they are, or what they do—it's for the common good.

PLATO

CONTRIBUTING, OR GIVING, TO THE COMMON GOOD OF YOUR COMMUNITY CAN BE AS EASY AS MOWING A NEIGHBOR'S LAWN OR VOLUNTEERING AT AN ANIMAL SHELTER.

CITIZENS IN ACTION

FOR THE ANCIENT GREEK THINKER PLATO, THE COMMON GOOD WAS WHEN ALL PEOPLE LIVED WELL TOGETHER AND WORKED TOWARD A COMMON GOAL IN BOTH **POLITICS** AND SOCIETY. EVEN WHEN PEOPLE DISAGREE, THEY SHOULD STILL BE ABLE TO WORK TOGETHER.

GOOD FOR ALL

In order for the common good to work, it must be the same for every person in a society or community. This means the common good must apply to everyone equally and in all **situations**.

If something is good for one group of people but not another, then it can't be considered common. This is why the common good is so important to a community. When something benefits, or is good, for a community, it should apply to everyone!

PICKING UP TRASH IN YOUR COMMUNITY BENEFITS EVERYONE. THIS IS A GREAT WAY TO CONTRIBUTE TO THE COMMON GOOD. ▶

WHO DECIDES?

The common good is usually decided when the people of a community come together to talk about important issues. Some communities elect leaders who help decide what the common good is by passing laws that reflect their beliefs.

In some cases, however, an individual might decide. Think about your classroom, where your teacher decides what the common good is. This is because your teacher has more knowledge about the world, which allows them to make better decisions about your classroom's common good.

GEORGE WASHINGTON

MANY OF OUR NATION'S IDEAS ABOUT THE COMMON GOOD ARE FOUND IN THE U.S. CONSTITUTION. THE CONSTITUTION CONTINUES TO HAVE A SAY IN OUR COUNTRY'S COMMON GOOD.

U.S. CONSTITUTION

CITIZENS IN ACTION

GEORGE WASHINGTON AND HIS GOVERNMENT WROTE AND **ENACTED** THE FIRST LAWS OF THE UNITED STATES, WHICH HELPED DEFINE THE COMMON GOOD FOR GENERATIONS TO COME.

GET THE WORD OUT

For people to believe the common good is actually good for everyone, it needs to be promoted. "Promotion" is when a person or group provides active **support** for a cause.

Think about the commercials you see on television. Those are promotions for products, or goods, companies want you to buy or movies they want you to see. Companies must actively try and let other people know why they think their product or message is important. The same can be done for the common good.

IN ORDER FOR STORES, GROUPS, OR EVEN INDIVIDUALS TO GET THE WORD OUT ON SOMETHING IMPORTANT, THEY MUST PROMOTE IT. ▶

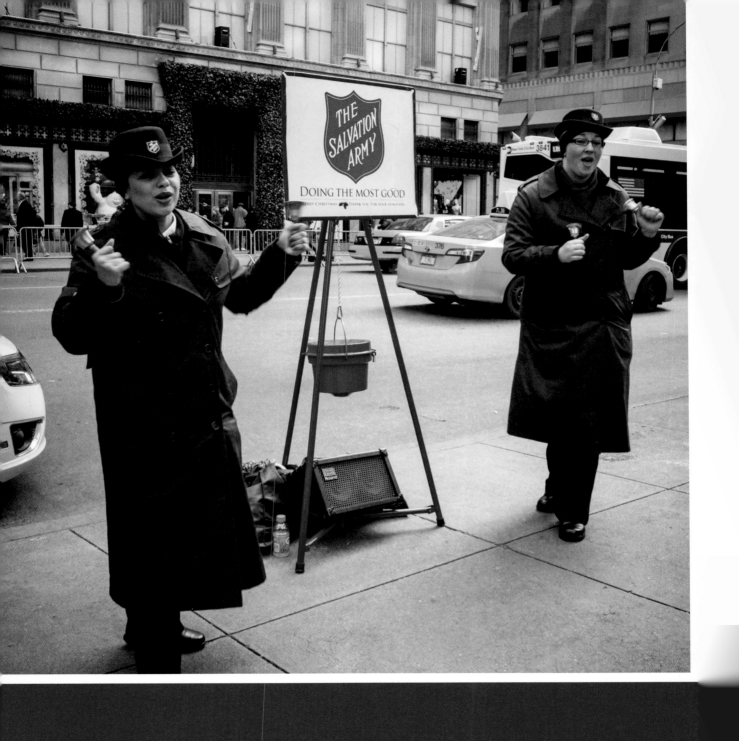

PROMOTED BY THE PEOPLE

The common good can be harder to promote than a new computer or a sale at a fancy store. This is because the idea of the common good is **abstract**. Because of this, it's important to promote the common good in a way that everyone can understand.

Ordinary people must also help **politicians** or community leaders in the promotion. People must come together to help promote the common good, otherwise communities might not believe it's good for everyone.

PROMOTING THE COMMON GOOD REQUIRES ORDINARY CITIZENS TO COME TOGETHER TO HELP PROMOTE IT. THE MORE PEOPLE PROMOTING THE COMMON GOOD, THE EASIER IT IS TO GET OTHERS TO BELIEVE IN IT.

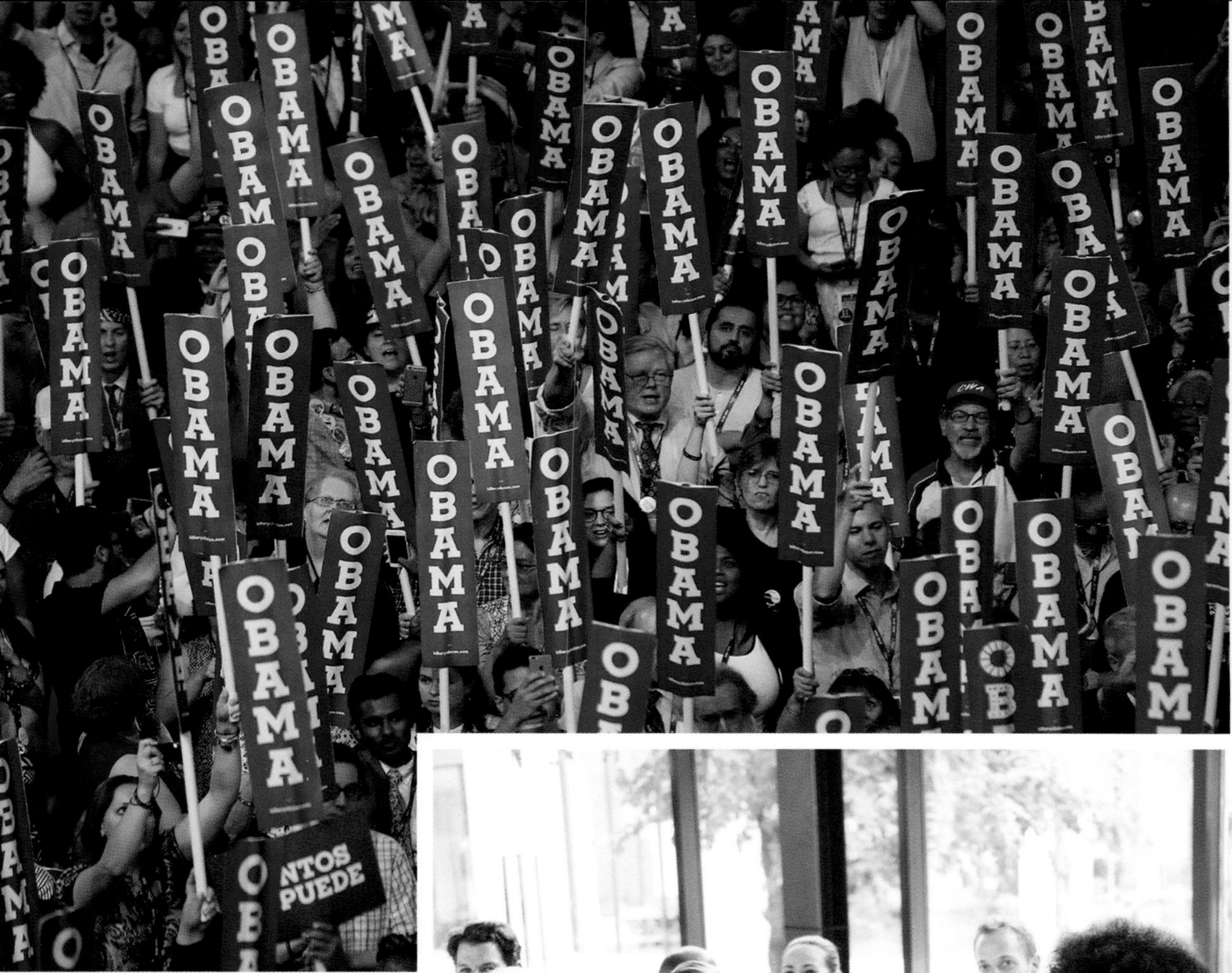
OBAMA

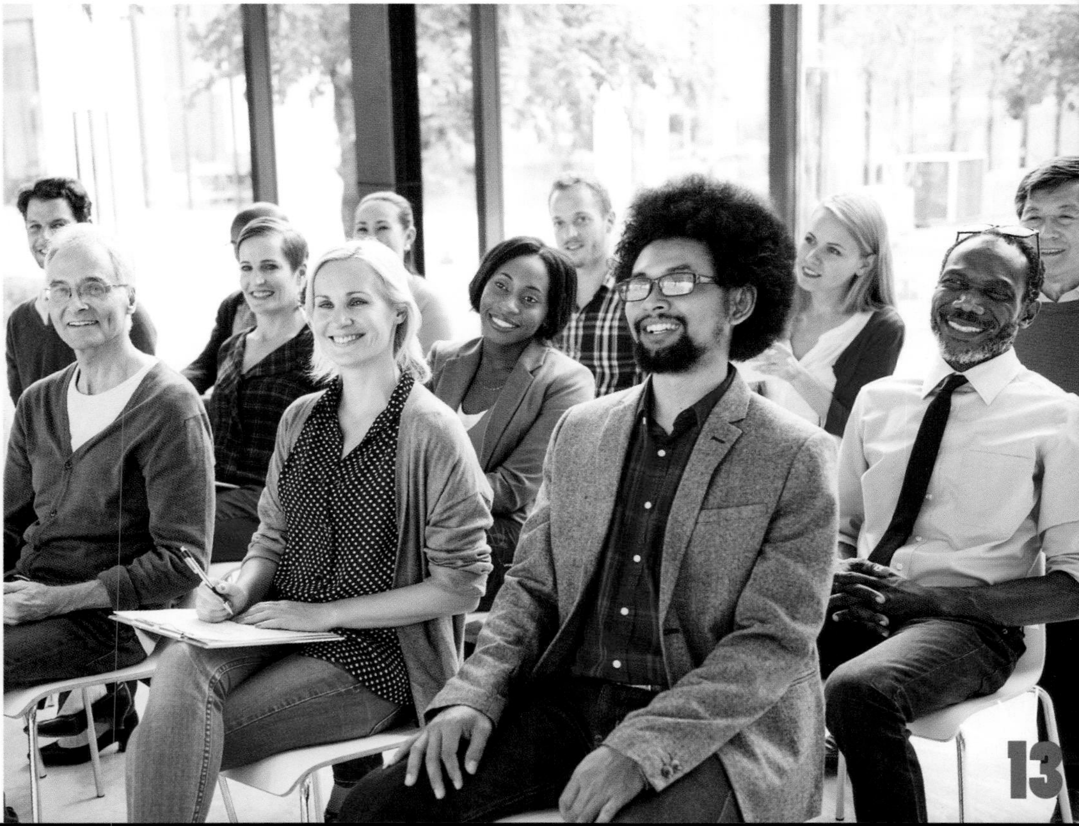

THE U.S. COMMON GOOD

You might think having a common good for a country as large as the United States is hard, and you would be correct! However, there are a few values that help form our common good.

We believe that each person has the right to life, liberty, and the **pursuit** of happiness. Our common good centers on people's individual right to live a happy life as they see fit, as long as it doesn't stop other people from doing the same.

THE UNITED STATES' COMMON GOOD HAS BEEN SHAPED BY BOTH CITIZENS AND GREAT LEADERS AND THINKERS.

HOW CAN YOU HELP?

As a young person, it might feel like there's little you can do to promote the common good. However, once you have a good understanding of what the common good is, there are many ways you can get **involved**.

Have a bake sale where you donate, or give, the money to a cause you care about. Talk to adults about a law you'd like to see passed. Write a report about something that's important to you. There's lots you can do to promote the common good.

THERE ARE MANY WAYS FOR STUDENTS AND YOUNG PEOPLE TO HELP PROMOTE THE COMMON GOOD. ALL IT TAKES IS A LITTLE DRIVE AND HARD WORK FOR YOUR VOICE TO BE HEARD.

17

CHANGING THE COMMON GOOD

In the United States, ideas about the common good have changed over time. When the nation was founded, slavery was allowed and considered a good thing for the country. Eventually, enough people believed slavery was bad and it was made illegal.

There are many ways to change the common good, but most involve changing laws or changing the way people think. This can be done through **activism**, voting for **representatives** who share your values, running for office, or simply by talking with people about important issues.

THE 1950s WERE A TIME OF GREAT CHANGE FOR CIVIL RIGHTS IN THE UNITED STATES. SHOWN HERE IS A VOTER REGISTRATION DRIVE FROM 1952 ATTENDED BY BLACK PEOPLE AND WHITE PEOPLE, AS WELL AS MEN AND WOMEN.

CITIZENS IN ACTION

ABOLITIONISTS, OR PEOPLE WHO FOUGHT TO END SLAVERY, PLAYED A HUGE PART IN CHANGING THE COMMON GOOD IN EARLY AMERICA. THESE WERE ORDINARY CITIZENS WHO HELPED SLAVES ESCAPE THEIR MASTERS AND FOUGHT TO HAVE THE LAWS CHANGED.

THE BEST FOR EVERYONE

So now you know what the common good is. You also know how to promote it and even how to change it. But why is this important?

Living in a society is about more than wanting what's best for yourself. It's also about what's best for your neighbor, your community, your country, and even the rest of the world. The only way to make sure this happens is by promoting the common good and talking with people who might have different opinions.

PUBLIC **DEBATES**—FROM PRESIDENTS TO LOCAL ACTIVISTS—HAVE BEEN VERY IMPORTANT IN HELPING SHAPE THE COMMON GOOD IN THE UNITED STATES.

YOUR COMMUNITY NEEDS YOU!

One reason why the common good may not be known to as many people as it should be is because so many depend on other people to do the work. Your community needs citizens like you to step up and help out.

Whether it's your classroom, your town, or even your state, your community needs you to do your part in promoting the common good. When citizens work together, they can create positive change that benefits everyone.

GLOSSARY

abstract: A thought or idea that isn't connected to a physical object.

activism: Acting strongly in support of or against an issue.

debate: A meeting at which different people or groups argue different points of view.

enact: To make something an official part of the law.

involve: To take part in something.

politician: A person who holds or runs for a government position.

politics: The science of government and elections.

pursuit: The act of trying to get or to seek something.

representative: One who stands for a group of people; a member of a lawmaking body who acts for voters.

situation: All the facts, conditions, and events that affect someone or something in a certain time and place.

support: To hold up and help.

INDEX

WEBSITES

Due to the changing nature of Internet links, PowerKids Press has developed an
online list of websites related to the subject of this book. This site is updated regularly.
Please use this link to access the list: www.powerkidslinks.com/civicv/promo